Disclaimer Notice

This book belongs to:

"Come on, **Lucas!** We are going to be late!"
"Honey... let's get down now."

Lucas's parents asked him to get downstairs.

"Let me get him," Mike calmed Sarah. Oscar whimpered pacing around the kitchen.

Avoiding school, missing buses and forgetting lunch for school had become a usual morning for the family. Sarah and Mike had been worried about **Lucas's** behavior for the past few weeks. He was constantly irritated, worried and throwing fits. He seemed to be in his own head.
Mike knocked on the half-opened door and pushed it open gently.

Lucas was sitting on his bed with his arms crossed, facing the wall, all dressed up for school. He seemed to be mad.

Mike sits on the bed
with him, moves his hand
on his back and asks,

**What's going on, buddy?
Are you feeling okay?**

"I do not know,"
mumbled Lucas without looking up.

Mike held **Lucas's** little hands and looked into his eyes, "Clearly, there is something going on, Lucas. Even if you do not know why you are feeling a certain way, tell me anything on your mind, and we will sort it out together."

"I do not want to go to school. What if Ms. Patricia asks me to read? What if it rains again? I do not want to get my shoes wet again... I am mad about the day you took Oscar to the vet. He did not like it."

"Luca bubba... come here," Mike sighed in relief and put his arms out. "I understand you feel angry and irritated, but there are a lot of ifs and dids. You cannot change anything about them."

Lucas slid away and asked curiously,

"What are ifs and dids?"

"Well, ifs is something that you think will happen and has just about no ground in reality. **What if I fail? What if my friend is no longer my friend? What if zombies destroy my school,** " Mike tickled Lucas imitating a zombie.

"And dids is what happened in the past and what you cannot change. I failed my exam. I could not goal, or I spilt syrup on my shirt."

Lucas hugged Mike back with confused eyes. "Tell you what! Let's skip school. I have a surprise for you." Mike stood up, holding Lucas's hand.

"Hey, baby. Are you okay?" asked Sarah as Luca came downstairs. He nodded his head, squinting his eyes and pushing the glasses up with his hand.

Sarah hugged Lucas. **"Luca** and I are taking a trip to the park. We need to chat a bit," Mike winked at Sarah smiling.

"Wow. That's so fun! It is getting cloudy. **Why don't you take the umbrella?"** said Sarah sipping coffee as **Lucas** ran to Mike.

Mike got down on his knees and said, "You see? Mommy just had a what-if thought, and she handled it so good. That is what you do about the what-ifs instead of
worrying about them. You find a solution for them."

"Hmm, I see what you are talking about... dad's right **Luca,** but this what-if thought had some base. Clouds show that it could rain. **Remember not to pay attention to everything that comes to your mind,"** explained Sarah handing **Luca** the umbrella and smiling.

Mike and **Lucas** headed to the park, saying goodbye to Sarah, jumping over puddles swinging arms.

"Lucas do you feel better now?" asked Mike.

"I think so, yes," replied **Lucas** vaguely.

"Let's play a game!" exclaimed Mike, "Tell me five things you can see!""Umm, I see you..." replied Lucas thinking and jumping.

"That's right, bubba! Now concentrate. Tell me more," said Mike playfully.

"You, that tree, my feet, the clouds and... the floor!" answered **Lucas** observing everything left and right.

"Good Job!" exclaimed Mike, **"Now give me four things you can hear! You can do it."**

"Okay. Okay," **Lucas giggled**. "I can hear...those kids running, the sound of that car, the guitarist over there and.." responded Lucas pointing here and there, thinking. "The birds bubba. Don't you hear them singing? They sound beautiful, right?" described Mike.

Oh yes, the birds! I did not hear them at all!" **Lucas** looked up at the little sparrows and hummingbirds chirping on the tall trees as they shed leaves on **Lucas's** face.

"Wow!" Lucas jumped with joy.
"Okay, now three things you can smell. This one can be hard, but I know you will do it," said Mike smiling as they entered the park.
"What do I smell...? I smell something funny!" responded **Lucas** putting his hand to his nose.
"You are right! Looks like some animal decided to do their business here... " Mike covered his nose disgustedly, looking at poo near the bushes.
Lucas ran ahead at full speed.

"Hey, Lucas! Do not go too far! Wait, I'm coming!" shouted Mike catching up.
"Ahhh!" Lucas smiled, sniffing rose flowers, "I came to smell the flowers, dad! I do not like that **yucky smell."**

"Oh, there you go! You have found another smell!" laughed Mike gasping with his hands on his knees. "I smell food too, dad..." mumbled Lucas looking around as a lady walked by him with a croissant at some distance.
"You got it, bubba!" he exclaimed excitedly.
"Now give me two things you can touch," added Mike. Lucas sat on the ground tiredly.

"I am touching this grass," Lucas moved his hand on the green grass with his little hands.

"I am touching myself. Does that count?" asked Lucas, looking up to Mike, touching his arm as the Sun glared in his glasses."Yes! It does! You are so good at it, Lucas. Good boy!" said Mike, sitting down happily, "There is only one challenge left, then you win!"

"What, dad? What?" asked Luca curiously. "You have to name one thing you can taste right now!"

"O...umm... I can still taste the sandwich mum made me. Does that count?" asked Lucas, moving his tongue around his mouth.

"You are silly!" laughed Mike, "Let's get up and sit by the lake. I need to tell you a story."

"What story, dad?" Luca got up quickly.
"The game we have just played. It is the favorite game of a dragon. I am going to tell you his story," explained Mike. **"Woah, a dragon?" Lucas** held Mike's hand excitedly.

Hand in hand, the father-son duo walked towards the blue lake, home to the majestic swans calling and ducks flashing their radiant colors as they dived in the water for breakfast. The birds and the Sun seemed to exchange greetings after a long cold night.

Lucas and Mike sat on the bench under the big old orange oak tree, bidding farewell to its precious leaves. They saw the Sun in all its glory overlooking the lake.

"Lucas, before I start the story, I want to tell you the point of our conversation. I love you so much, and mum, your teachers and I feel you are not feeling okay. You do not play with your friends anymore, and you cannot focus on your lessons anymore. You get worried about little things and enjoy very little," explained Mike, concerned.

Lucas sat with his head down, fidgeting all of a sudden sad again.

"It's okay. Everyone feels like this at times. I do too.

We have so many thoughts in a day. Scientists say that we have at least one thought every two seconds. That is about 40000 thoughts a day! We cannot control the thoughts that come into our heads, and they usually come and go on their own.
You can think of thoughts like bubbles. They come, get bigger, and they pop, but some bubbles do not pop; instead, they keep on getting bigger and bigger. They take up all the space in your brain, and you cannot think of anything else.

Your brain gets full like an answering machine. Until you get rid of old messages, you cannot get new ones! Will you not be missing important messages and the ones that need to be responded to quickly?

So, when you are constantly worried about things that might happen in the future or have happened in the past and are unchangeable, your brain gets full of useless thoughts. Useless thoughts make you sad, **worried and angry!**

You start living in the past or the future. You miss out on all the fun things about the present and ways you can make your future problems away or wishes true!"

Lucas was looking up at Mike, so confused.

"I know it can be hard to understand,"said Mike, smiling at Lucas's innocence. "Let's hear the story first and go from there."

"Thousands of years ago, a gigantic mysterious forest of coast redwoods was hiding underneath a big circle of pointy orange mountains. The hundreds of deep caves inside these mountains were home to the fire-breathing flying dragons.
In one of those caves lived Aidan with his mother, Edna, the Queen of all dragons. Aidan was a grey-scaled dragon with green eyes and little teeth. The fiery red Queen had raised him alone after the king died and took responsibility for protecting the kingdom.
Aidan had always been the child who worried a bit too much. He was turning 10 that year. Normally, all dragons in the Circle started to fly by that age. Most dragons did it on their own, but some needed a little nudge.

Aidan was too scared to even try because he was consumed by his own thoughts. He was afraid he would fall or, at best, he would not be a good flyer. And what is a Queen's son and a future king of the kingdom who could not even fly, right?

He was so much stuck in his thoughts to actually learn how to fly. He would not listen to the Queen or anyone who gave him advice about flying. His mind always wandered around the future where he could not fly, and the kingdom was at a lost because of him.

The Queen was concerned for him. His wings had started to lose their strength, so even when the Queen pushed him to fly, he could not flap his wings. He started staying in the cave even more and did not have any friends. He had convinced himself that he would not be able to fly.

So, on his 17th birthday, the Queen took him to the forest and gave him a ride. She told him

'You are not your thoughts Aidan. You cannot control which thoughts you have, but you can choose which thoughts to carry forward. If you keep worrying about the future or past things, you lose the present.

It is a must to feel and live the present as it is all you truly have.

Close your eyes. Open your wings. Feel the air that touches them and tell yourself you can fly. Leave the worries behind as you fly away from them.'

Are you following bubba?"
Mike narrated.

Lucas, so focused on the story, was holding Mike's hand and looking up at him.

"I do, dad, but I need to know how Aidan made his worries go away. Did he fly at the end, dad?" inquired Lucas curiously.

"Oh yes, he did, Lucas. He became the greatest dragon king anyone had seen at the Circle. He flew so brilliantly that dragons from faraway lands came just to see him flying. And you know what?

He was a grey-scaled dragon, but when he stopped fixating on his thought and started to be present in the moment, the color of his scales changed into the most beautiful blue.

His wings grew so strong and the biggest of them all.

His brain was so tired of thinking the same useless thoughts repeatedly that he could not focus and learn to be the greatest dragon.

You want to know how he stayed in the present. Right?

Let me show you," smiled Mike.

The Queen showed Aidan how he could let go of his worries to make the most of life and be his best self.

Let's try with Aidan

Lie down in a comfortable position. *Imagine having a balloon in your stomach. Imagine the balloon slowly expanding as you inhale. The balloon effortlessly deflates as you exhale.* **You can place your favorite toy on your stomach and take them for a peaceful journey.**

Make sure you tell yourself something positive about yourself every day. Pick at least three of the following for each day:

I am smart, amazing, and powerful.
I can do more than I believe.
I don't need to worry. I can try again.
My dreams will come true.
My heart is full of courage and kindness.
I am great today. I will be even greater tomorrow.
I am worthy.
I can create my life just the way I want it.
I love myself.
I am happy.
Every day my life and I are better and better.
Learning is fun!
I overcome challenges easily.

I am unique.
I am thankful and happy for everything I have and am.
I love the world around me.
I am optimistic every day.
Everything I do matters.
I am powerful and courageous.
My family and friends are always there for me.

You can improve your awareness of what is happening inside of you and around you by occasionally reminding yourself to pause during the day.

S

Stop
What you are **Doing**
for a Second.

T

Take a breath. Notice how you
are **Breathing.** The Breath is an
Anchor for the Present.

O

Observe. Take note of what is happening. What is happening inside
you and outside of you? Where did
your mind go? How are you feeling?
What are you doing?

P

Proceed. Continue what you
were doing.

Close your eyes.
Think of something that makes you **Happy.**
Sketch it in a **Notebook with some Crayons.**
Think about how the Crayon feels in your Hand.
Think about how the Paper Feels.
Think about why you are Choosing Certain Colors for your **Drawing.**
Explain out loud what you are Drawing.

Imagine you are sitting in a **Magical Meadow.**
Imagine your **favorite flower** blooming in the grass.
Relax as you see the flower growing.

What color is your flower?
What does it look like?
What do you think it will smell like?

Pay **attention and breathe deeply.**
Notice how your body feels.
Stoop down and slowly pick up the flower.
Take a deep breath in and enjoy the flower's smell.
Breathe out and blow the tiny petals away.

Jump for **30 seconds.**
Sit down and close your eyes.
Place a hand over your heart.
Feel your heartbeat for **15 seconds.**

Go on a **Scavenger hunt.**

Make a list of what you need to **look for outside.**
You can look for a plant, a butterfly, an s-shaped
object, and a bird singing. Anything at all you want.

**Stroll around the yard, field, block, or neighbor-
hood park; take your time to look for the items.**

Thoughts are words we say to ourselves.

We have thoughts all the time, most of the time without even us realizing it.

Two people can have different thoughts about the same thing.

You do not need to respond to every thought that comes to your mind.

If a thought makes you worried about your future, think of a solution for the problem. If there is no solution to that problem, blow the thought away.

If a thought makes you sad or angry about something which happened in the past, blow it away.

Blow away thoughts about anything you have no control over.

When you are focused on the present, you can:

Enjoy and make happy moments.
Do not feel sad and angry.
Behave responsibly.
Be a better friend.
Understand and take care of yourself.
Understand and take care of others.

www.ingramcontent.com/pod-product-compliance
Lightning Source LLC
Chambersburg PA
CBHW041554120626
46551CB00002B/204